3

rocker girl tutu and t-shirt

Our model is wearing a 10" long tutu.

SHOPPING LIST

TUTU

EITHER LENGTH TUTU:
- ☐ 1½ yards of 1½" wide black satin ribbon for waist tie
- ☐ assorted sizes clear acrylic jewels
- ☐ low temp glue gun and glue sticks

10" LONG TUTU:
- ☐ 10 yards **each** of 6" wide dark pink metallic dot and black/pink dot tulle
- ☐ 3½ yards of ⅝" wide black/white zebra print ribbon

18" LONG TUTU:
- ☐ 18 yards **each** of 6" wide dark pink metallic dot and black/pink dot tulle
- ☐ 6 yards of ⅝" wide black/white zebra print ribbon

T-SHIRT
- ☐ black T-shirt
- ☐ rhinestone iron-on design

To make the Rocker Girl Tutu and T-shirt:

Refer to the General Instructions, page 30, when making the tutu.

For the tutu, use tulle to make a *Basic Tutu*, alternating the dark pink and black tulle strips and adding the zebra print ribbons as desired. Glue the rhinestones to the tulle as desired.

For the T-shirt, follow the manufacturer's instructions to apply the rhinestone design to the T-shirt.

5

birthday girl ensemble

Our model is wearing an 18" long tutu.

SHOPPING LIST

TUTU

EITHER LENGTH TUTU:
- [ ] 1½ yards of 1½" wide hot pink satin ribbon for waist tie

10" LONG TUTU:
- [ ] 5 yards **each** of 6" wide green glitter dot, aqua glitter dot, yellow glitter dot, dark pink glitter dot, and pink glitter dot tulle

18" LONG TUTU:
- [ ] 9 yards **each** of 6" wide green glitter dot, aqua glitter dot, yellow glitter dot, dark pink glitter dot, and pink glitter dot tulle

T-SHIRT
- [ ] four 5" lengths of 6" wide dark pink glitter dot tulle
- [ ] two 6" lengths of ³/₈" wide pink ribbon
- [ ] light pink T-shirt
- [ ] felt butterflies
- [ ] clear acrylic jewels
- [ ] fabric glue

PARTY HAT
- [ ] ³/₄ yard **each** of 6" wide green glitter dot, aqua glitter dot, yellow glitter dot, dark pink glitter dot, and pink glitter dot tulle
- [ ] decorative cardstock
- [ ] aqua fabric-covered headband
- [ ] ¼" dia. hole punch
- [ ] tape
- [ ] tracing paper
- [ ] low temp glue gun and glue sticks

CAKE STAND TUTU
- [ ] 2¼ yards **each** of 6" wide green glitter dot, aqua glitter dot, yellow glitter dot, dark pink glitter dot, and pink glitter dot tulle
- [ ] embroidery floss to match tulle
- [ ] pink chenille stems
- [ ] cake stand

GARLAND
- [ ] 2 yards of 6" wide tulle per pom-pom (we made 13 pom-poms for our 72" long garland)
- [ ] 12" of ¹/₈" wide ribbon per pom-pom to match tulle
- [ ] desired length of ⁵/₈" wide ribbon for garland

To make the Birthday Girl Ensemble:

Refer to the General Instructions, pages 30-31, when making the tutu and pom-poms.

For the tutu, use the tulle to make a *Basic Tutu*, alternating colors as desired. Knot the tulle ends.

For the T-shirt, glue the butterflies to the T-shirt; glue the jewels to the butterflies. For each shoulder bow, gather and tie the centers of two dark pink tulle lengths together with a ribbon length; trim the ribbon ends. Glue the bows to the T-shirt shoulders.

Continued on page 8.

birthday girl continued

For the party hat, trace the pattern (page 25) onto tracing paper and cut out. Use the pattern to cut the hat from the cardstock. Insert the tab into the slit and tape on the inside. Punch 24-25 holes around the hat bottom. Cut tulle into 4" lengths. Pinch a tulle piece at the center and insert in a hole on the hat; glue in place. Repeat for the remaining holes along the hat bottom. Repeat with the remaining tulle pieces, inserting them into the hat top; glue in place from the inside. Trim the tulle ends as desired. Glue the hat to the headband.

For the cake stand tutu, twist the chenille stems together to make a circle that will fit around the cake stand base. Cut 16" tulle lengths. Loop the tulle lengths over the chenille stem circle and tie with matching floss *(Fig. 1)*; trim the floss ends to about ¹/₂". Trim the tulle ends as desired. Slide the tutu onto the cake stand base.

Fig. 1

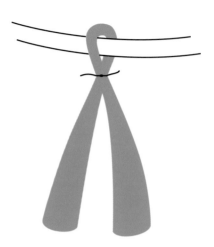

For each pom-pom on the garland, cut twelve 6" lengths of tulle. Stack the pieces and make a *Basic Pom-Pom.* Trim the pom-poms as desired. Tie the pom-poms to the garland ribbon as desired.

fanny pouf

Our model is wearing a 5" long pouf.

To make the Fanny Pouf:

Tie a double or triple knot about 15" from each end of the ribbon. Cut the tulle into 10" lengths. Referring to photo 4, page 30, knot the tulle lengths onto the ribbon between the knots.

forest fairy ensemble

Our model is wearing an 18" long tutu.

SHOPPING LIST

TUTU

EITHER LENGTH TUTU:
- ☐ 1½ yards of 1" wide yellow grosgrain ribbon for waist tie

10" LONG TUTU:
- ☐ 5¾ yards **each** of 6" wide aqua glitter, yellow glitter dot, green glitter, and orange glitter dot tulle

18" LONG TUTU:
- ☐ 10 yards **each** of 6" wide aqua glitter, yellow glitter dot, green glitter, and orange glitter dot tulle

FLOWERED HEAD RING
- ☐ 1 yard **each** of 6" wide aqua glitter, yellow glitter dot, and orange glitter dot tulle
- ☐ 1¾ yards of 6" wide green glitter tulle
- ☐ 1 yard of 1" wide yellow grosgrain ribbon
- ☐ 2¼ yards of ¼" wide orange satin ribbon
- ☐ green chenille stems
- ☐ 8 silk daisies
- ☐ low temp glue gun and glue sticks

WINGS
- ☐ ½ yard **each** of 6" wide aqua glitter, yellow glitter dot, green glitter, and orange glitter dot tulle
- ☐ 12" length of 1" wide yellow grosgrain ribbon
- ☐ ½ yard of ¼" wide orange satin ribbon
- ☐ 11" wide x 10" high fairy wings or a nylon butterfly (we found ours in the home décor dept. of the craft store)
- ☐ adhesive back hook and loop fastener tape
- ☐ silk daisy
- ☐ fabric glue
- ☐ low temp glue gun and glue sticks

WAND
- ☐ 24" length **each** of 6" wide yellow glitter dot, green glitter, and orange glitter dot tulle
- ☐ 1⅜ yards of 6" wide aqua glitter tulle
- ☐ 1 yard of ¼"w orange satin ribbon
- ☐ 24" of ⅛"w orange satin ribbon
- ☐ 12" long ¼" dia. dowel
- ☐ orange acrylic paint and paintbrush
- ☐ silk daisy
- ☐ low temp glue gun and glue sticks

To make the Forest Fairy Ensemble:

Refer to the General Instructions, pages 30-31, when making the tutu and pom-poms.

For the tutu, use the tulle to make a *Basic Tutu,* alternating colors as desired. Knot the tulle ends.

Continued on page 12.

For the flowered head ring, twist the ends together to join the chenille stems into a ring that will sit on your child's head. For the streamers, cut an 18" length of each color tulle; set aside. Loosely wrap the ring with the remaining green tulle, gluing in place as necessary. Tie the streamers to the ring with a 20" orange ribbon length. Glue a yellow ribbon bow over the orange ribbon. Cut the remaining tulle into 4" lengths; cut nine 12" lengths of orange ribbon. Gather and tie each tulle length at the center with an orange ribbon length; trim the ribbon ends to about $1/2$". Remove the daisies from the stems. Glue the daisies and gathered tulle pieces to the ring. Trim the tulle streamer and ribbon ends as desired.

For the wings, stack the tulle lengths; gather and tie at the center with the orange ribbon. Remove the daisy from the stem. Use the low temp glue gun to glue the gathered tulle, a yellow ribbon bow, and the daisy to the wings. Trim the tulle and ribbon ends as desired. Use the low temp glue gun to glue the hook side of the fastener to the wings. Use the fabric glue to glue the loop side to the shirt back.

For the wand, cut the aqua tulle piece into eight 6" long lengths; cut the remaining tulle pieces into four 6" lengths each. To make each pom-pom, use 4 aqua pieces and 2 pieces each of the other colors to make a *Basic Pom-Pom*. Make 2 pom-poms, trimming the $1/8$"wide ribbon ends to about $1/2$". Paint the dowel. When dry, glue the pom-poms back to back to one end of the dowel. Cut the $1/4$"wide ribbon in half and tie around the dowel; glue in place. Remove the daisy from the stem and glue to the wand.

dolly tutu

Fits an 18" tall doll.

SHOPPING LIST

- ☐ 2 yards **each** of 6" wide dark pink glitter dot, purple glitter, and lavender glitter tulle
- ☐ 1¼ yards **each** of ⅛" wide light pink, purple, and lavender ribbon
- ☐ ¾ yard of ⅝" wide pink satin ribbon for waist tie

To make the Dolly Tutu:

Tie a double or triple knot about 7½" from each end of the waist tie ribbon. Cut the tulle into 10" lengths and the ribbon into 6" lengths. Loop the tulle lengths over the waist tie between the knots and tie with the 6" ribbon lengths *(Fig. 1)*; trim the ribbon ends to about ½". Trim the tulle ends as desired.

Fig. 1

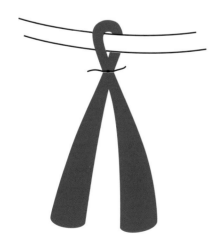

13

princess ensemble

Our model is wearing an 18" long tutu.

SHOPPING LIST

TUTU

EITHER LENGTH TUTU:
- ☐ 1½ yards of 1½" wide pink satin ribbon for waist tie

10" LONG TUTU:
- ☐ 5 yards **each** of 6" wide dark pink glitter dot, light pink glitter dot, purple glitter, and lavender glitter tulle

18" LONG TUTU:
- ☐ 9 yards **each** of 6" wide dark pink glitter dot, light pink glitter dot, purple glitter, and lavender glitter tulle

SHOES

- ☐ 12" **each** of 6" wide dark pink glitter dot, light pink glitter dot, and purple glitter tulle
- ☐ 24" of ⅛"w dark pink satin ribbon
- ☐ 2 pink acrylic jewels
- ☐ low temp glue gun and glue sticks

HAT

- ☐ ½ yard **each** of 6" wide dark pink glitter dot, light pink glitter dot, purple sparkle, and lavender glitter tulle
- ☐ decorative cardstock
- ☐ dark pink fabric-covered headband
- ☐ 4 pink acrylic jewels
- ☐ tracing paper
- ☐ tape
- ☐ low temp glue gun and glue sticks

WAND

- ☐ 24" **each** of 6" wide dark pink glitter dot, light pink glitter dot, purple glitter, and lavender glitter tulle
- ☐ ⅝ yard of ⅝"w dark pink satin ribbon
- ☐ 24" of ⅛"w dark pink satin ribbon
- ☐ ¾ yard of silver wired cord
- ☐ 12" long ¼" dia. dowel
- ☐ pink acrylic paint and paintbrush
- ☐ low temp glue gun and glue sticks

To make the Princess Ensemble:

Refer to the General Instructions, pages 30-31, when making the tutu and pom-poms.

For the tutu, use the tulle to make a *Basic Tutu*, alternating colors as desired. Trim the tulle ends as desired.

For the hat, trace the pattern (page 25) onto tracing paper and cut out. Use the pattern to cut the hat from the cardstock. Insert the tab into the slit and tape on the inside. Wrap the lavender tulle around the hat bottom edge, gathering and gluing in place at the imaginary four "corners" of the circle. Cut four 2" purple tulle lengths; gather and glue over the gathered areas of lavender tulle. Glue the jewels to the purple tulle. Thread the remaining tulle lengths through the hat top (from the inside) and glue. Trim the tulle ends as desired. Glue the hat to the headband.

Continued on page 16.

For the shoes, cut each tulle piece into two 6" long strips. For each pom-pom, use 1 piece of each color tulle to make a Basic Pom-Pom. Make 2 pom-poms, trimming the $1/8$"wide ribbon ends to about $1/2$". Glue the pompoms to the shoes; glue the jewels to the pom-poms.

For the wand, cut each tulle piece into four 6" lengths; cut the silver cord into four $6^3/4$" lengths. To make each pom-pom, use 2 pieces of each color tulle and 2 pieces of silver cord to make a *Basic Pom-Pom*. Make 2 pompoms, trimming the $1/8$" wide ribbon ends to about $1/2$". Paint the dowel. When dry, glue the pom-poms back to back to one end of the dowel. Tie the dark pink ribbon in a bow around the dowel and glue in place.

tutu ponytail holder

To make the Hairwear:

Refer to the General Instructions, page 31, when making the pom-pom.

For the ponytail holder, cut a 3" length of tulle and set aside. Cut ten 6" lengths from the remaining lavender tulle and make a *Basic Pom-Pom*. Fold the 3" tulle length into a 1" x 3" piece, thread through the ponytail holder, and glue the ends to the pom-pom *(Fig. 1)*. Glue the embellishment to the pom-pom center.

Fig. 1

jungle girl ensemble

Our model is wearing a 10" long tutu.

SHOPPING LIST

TUTU

EITHER LENGTH TUTU:
- ☐ 1½ yards of 1½" wide brown satin ribbon for waist tie

10" LONG TUTU:
- ☐ 9½ yards **each** of 6" wide brown glitter and orange glitter dot tulle
- ☐ 3⅜ yards of ⅝" wide gold sheer ribbon
- ☐ 1¼ yards of 1½" wide leopard print ribbon

18" LONG TUTU:
- ☐ 17 yards **each** of 6" wide brown glitter and orange glitter dot tulle
- ☐ 6 yards of ⅝" wide gold sheer ribbon
- ☐ 2 yards of 1½" wide leopard print ribbon

TOP

- ☐ 22" square leopard print bandanna or 24" square of fabric
- ☐ 12" length **each** of 6" wide brown glitter and orange glitter dot tulle
- ☐ 2 yards of ⅞" wide black satin ribbon
- ☐ ½ yard of ⅝" wide gold sheer ribbon
- ☐ ⅞" wide paper-backed fusible web tape
- ☐ gold acrylic jewel
- ☐ fabric glue

HEADBAND

- ☐ 3⅜ yards **each** of 6" wide brown glitter and orange glitter dot tulle
- ☐ 4½ yards of ¼" wide brown satin ribbon
- ☐ brown fabric-covered headband
- ☐ low temp glue gun and glue sticks

WRISTLETS

- ☐ 1½ yards of 6" wide brown glitter tulle
- ☐ 24" of 6" wide orange glitter dot tulle
- ☐ 1¼ yards of ⅝" wide gold sheer ribbon
- ☐ 2 gold acrylic jewels
- ☐ low temp glue gun and glue sticks

BOOT TOPPERS

- ☐ 3½ yards **each** of 6" wide brown glitter and orange glitter dot tulle
- ☐ 1½ yards of ¼" wide brown satin ribbon
- ☐ embroidery floss to match tulle

To make the Jungle Girl Ensemble:
Refer to the General Instructions, pages 30-32, when making the tutu, pom-poms, and top.

For the tutu, use the tulle to make a *Basic Tutu*, alternating the orange and brown tulle strips and adding the ribbons as desired.

For the top, use the bandanna or fabric to make a *Basic Top*. Cut the tulle into 6" lengths. Stack the pieces and gather at the center; tie with a 12" length of gold ribbon. Glue the gathered tulle to the top. Glue two 3" gold ribbon lengths and the jewel to the tulle. Trim the ribbon ends as desired.

For the headband, cut twenty 6" lengths of each color of tulle and twenty 8" lengths of ribbon. Holding two of the same color together, lay the tulle lengths on the headband and secure by tying with a ribbon length; glue if necessary. Trim the ribbon ends to about $1/2$".

For each wristlet, cut four 6" lengths of brown tulle and two 6" lengths of orange tulle. Stack the pieces and make a *Basic Pom-Pom*, using a $22^{1}/_{2}$" length of the $5/8$" wide ribbon to tie the pom-pom; do not cut the ribbon ends. Glue a jewel to the pom-pom center.

For each boot topper, cut ten 6" lengths of each color tulle; cut the ribbon in half. Alternating colors, loop the tulle lengths over the ribbon and tie with floss *(Fig. 1)*. Trim the floss ends to about $1/2$".

Fig. 1

christmas tutu and t-shirt

Our model is wearing a 10" long tutu.

SHOPPING LIST

TUTU

EITHER LENGTH TUTU:
- [ ] 1½ yards of 1½" wide red satin ribbon for waist tie
- [ ] 2½ yards **each** of ⅛" wide red satin ribbon and ¼" wide white satin ribbon
- [ ] six 18mm green jingle bells
- [ ] low temp glue gun and glue sticks

10" LONG TUTU:
- [ ] 10 yards **each** of 6" wide white glitter, green glitter dot, and red glitter dot tulle

18" LONG TUTU:
- [ ] 18 yards **each** of 6" wide white glitter, green glitter dot, and red glitter dot tulle

T-SHIRT
- [ ] white T-shirt
- [ ] ¼ yard of 6" wide red glitter dot tulle
- [ ] 12" length of ⅜" wide red satin ribbon
- [ ] 9" length of ⅛" wide white satin ribbon
- [ ] 18mm green jingle bell
- [ ] iron-on letters
- [ ] red and white sewing thread
- [ ] tracing paper

To make the Christmas Tutu and T-shirt:
Refer to the General Instructions, page 30, when making the tutu.

For the tutu, use tulle to make a *Basic Tutu*, alternating the colors as desired. Cut the white and red ribbon into six 15" lengths. Holding one of each ribbon together, tie a bow, catching a bell in the knot. Tie six bows. Glue the bows to the tutu as desired.

For the T-shirt, trace the heart pattern onto tracing paper and cut out. Use the pattern to cut eight tulle hearts. Stack the tulle hearts and securely tack together at the center. Tie the white ribbon into a bow and tack to the tulle hearts. Tie the red ribbon into a bow, catching the bell in the knot. Arrange the red bow, letters, and heart on the T-shirt. Follow the manufacturer's instructions to adhere the letters; tack the bow and heart to the T-shirt.

Heart

witch ensemble

Our model is wearing an 18" long tutu.

SHOPPING LIST

TUTU

EITHER LENGTH TUTU:
- ☐ 1½ yards of 1½" wide orange satin ribbon for waist tie
- ☐ 2¾ yards of ⅜" wide green grosgrain ribbon
- ☐ 36" long ½" dia. dowel to curl the green ribbon
- ☐ clothespins
- ☐ decoupage glue
- ☐ disposable foam paintbrush
- ☐ low temp glue gun and glue sticks

10" LONG TUTU:
- ☐ 5 yards **each** of 6" wide green glitter dot, orange glitter dot, black glitter, and purple glitter tulle

18" LONG TUTU:
- ☐ 9 yards **each** of 6" wide green glitter dot, orange glitter dot, black glitter, and purple glitter tulle

HAT

- ☐ 1 yard **each** of 6" wide green glitter dot, orange glitter dot, and purple glitter tulle
- ☐ 1 yard of ⅜" wide green grosgrain ribbon
- ☐ 6" black felt witch hat
- ☐ green fabric-covered headband
- ☐ clear acrylic jewels
- ☐ low temp glue gun and glue sticks

TOP

- ☐ 22" square bandanna or 24" square of fabric
- ☐ 2½ yards of ⅞" wide orange satin ribbon
- ☐ ½ yard of ⅜" wide green grosgrain ribbon
- ☐ ⅞" wide paper-backed fusible web tape
- ☐ purple maribou feathers (cut a 3" length from a boa)
- ☐ jeweled/beaded spider embellishment
- ☐ fabric glue

BROOM

- ☐ 1 yard **each** of 6" wide green glitter dot and orange glitter dot tulle
- ☐ 2 yards **each** of 6" wide black glitter and purple glitter tulle
- ☐ 12" of ⅜"w green grosgrain ribbon
- ☐ 12" of ⅛"w black satin ribbon
- ☐ 36" long ½" dia. dowel
- ☐ clear acrylic jewel
- ☐ black acrylic paint and paintbrush
- ☐ low temp glue gun and glue sticks

Continued on page 24.

witch continued

To make the Witch Ensemble:

Refer to the General Instructions, pages 30 and 32, when making the tutu and top.

For the tutu, use the tulle to make a *Basic Tutu*, alternating colors as desired. Trim the tulle ends as desired. To make the curly ribbon streamers, cut five 20" lengths of green ribbon. Wrap the ribbons around the dowel, using clothespins to secure the ends. Apply decoupage glue to the ribbon with the foam brush and allow to dry. Remove the ribbons from the dowel and glue one end of each curly ribbon streamer to the tutu waist tie as desired.

For the hat, glue a ribbon band around the hat; glue jewels to the ribbon. To make the pouf, cut three 12" lengths from each color tulle. Stack the tulle lengths and tie with an 8" ribbon length. Glue the pouf to the hat. Tie a bow with the remaining ribbon and glue to the pouf. Trim the tulle and ribbon ends as desired. Glue the hat to the headband.

For the top, use the bandanna or fabric to make a *Basic Top*. Holding a 14" length of the green and orange ribbons together, tie the ribbons into a bow. Glue the feathers and spider to the bow; glue the bow to the top.

For the broom, paint the dowel black. Cut the tulle into 9" lengths. Alternating the colors as desired, tie the tulle to one dowel end with the black ribbon *(Fig. 1)*. Fold the tulle down over the end of the dowel *(Fig. 2)*. Wrap and glue the green ribbon around the tulle; glue the jewel to the ribbon. Trim the tulle and ribbon ends as desired.

Fig. 1

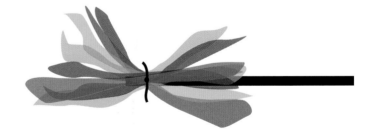

Fig. 2

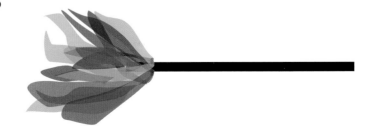

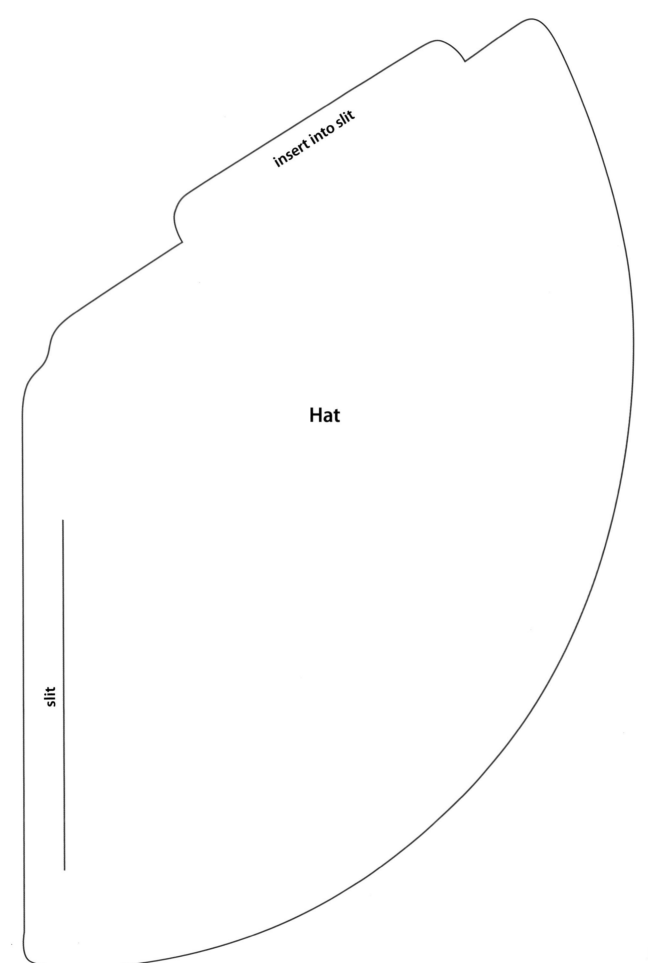

insert into slit

Hat

slit

camo girl tutu and headband

The mannequin is wearing a 10" long tutu.

SHOPPING LIST

TUTU

EITHER LENGTH TUTU:
- [ ] $1^1/_2$ yards of $1^1/_2$" wide pink satin ribbon for waist tie

10" LONG TUTU:
- [ ] 9 yards **each** of 6" wide pink glitter dot and brown glitter tulle
- [ ] $3^1/_2$ yards of $5/_8$" wide pink/brown dot grosgrain ribbon
- [ ] $1^1/_8$ yards of $1^1/_2$" wide pink camo print grosgrain ribbon

18" LONG TUTU:
- [ ] 16 yards **each** of 6" wide pink glitter dot and brown glitter tulle
- [ ] 6 yards of $5/_8$" wide pink/brown dot grosgrain ribbon
- [ ] 2 yards of $1^1/_2$" wide pink camo print grosgrain ribbon

HEADBAND

- [ ] $1^1/_4$ yards of 6" wide pink glitter dot tulle
- [ ] 1 yard of 6" wide brown glitter tulle
- [ ] $1/_2$ yard of $7/_8$" wide pink satin ribbon
- [ ] $5/_8$ yard of $1^1/_2$" wide pink camo print grosgrain ribbon
- [ ] 3 small pink silk daisies
- [ ] pink headband
- [ ] low temp glue gun and glue sticks

To make the Camo Girl Tutu and Headband:
Refer to the General Instructions, page 30, when making the tutu.

For the tutu, use the tulle to make a *Basic Tutu*, alternating the pink and brown tulle strips and adding the ribbons as desired.

For the headband, cut five 9" lengths of pink tulle; cut six 6" lengths of brown tulle. Stack the pink tulle pieces; center and stack the brown tulle pieces on the pink ones. Gather the tulle at the center and tie to the headband with the pink satin ribbon; tie a bow with the ribbon on the top of the headband. Tie a bow with the pink camo print ribbon; glue to the pink bow. Remove the daisies from the stems and glue to the bow.

blues tutu and headband

The mannequin is wearing a 10" long tutu.

SHOPPING LIST

TUTU

EITHER LENGTH TUTU:
- [ ] 1¹/₂ yards of 1¹/₂" wide blue satin ribbon for waist tie
- [ ] small blue/purple silk flowers
- [ ] low temp glue gun and glue sticks

10" LONG TUTU:
- [ ] 9 yards **each** of 6" wide blue glitter, purple glitter, and aqua glitter dot tulle

18" LONG TUTU:
- [ ] 16 yards **each** of 6" wide blue glitter, purple glitter, and aqua glitter dot tulle

HEADBAND

- [ ] ³/₄ yard of 6" wide blue glitter tulle
- [ ] 12" **each** of 6" wide purple glitter and aqua glitter dot tulle
- [ ] 3 small blue/purple trailing silk flower sprigs
- [ ] purple fabric-covered headband
- [ ] low temp glue gun and glue sticks

To make the Blues Tutu and Headband:

Refer to the General Instructions, page 30, when making the tutu.

For the tutu, use the tulle to make a *Basic Tutu*, alternating the colors as desired. Remove the flowers from the stems and glue to the tulle as desired.

For the headband, tie the purple and aqua tulle around the headband; glue in place. Tuck the flower sprigs into the tulle knot and glue in place. Tie the blue tulle into a bow and glue to the headband. Trim the tulle ends as desired.

general instructions

MAKING THE BASIC TUTU

These tutus are quick and easy to make. Because they tie on with ribbon, they'll fit sizes 2 to 8. You just need to decide the finished length, either 10" long or 18" long. Complete tulle and ribbon yardages for each length are given with each project.

To make the basic tutu, you'll need 1¹/₂" wide ribbon for the waist tie, 6" wide tulle on rolls (see individual projects for colors and amounts), tape measure, and scissors (photo 1).

To make cutting the tulle lengths easier, mark the work surface with tape pieces placed 20" apart for the shorter tutu or 36" apart for the longer tutu. Cut tulle strips the determined length (photo 2). If you are using ribbons in your tutu, cut them in the same manner.

Tie a double or triple knot about 15" from each end of waist tie (photo 3). The tulle and ribbon strips will be knotted onto the waist tie between the knots.

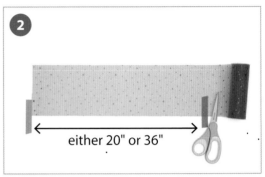

Fold a tulle length in half. Bring the tulle ends around the waist tie close to an end knot and pull the tulle ends through the loop (photo 4). Pull the knot snug.

Continue adding tulle lengths, pushing the pieces close together on the waist tie (photo 5). Ribbon lengths are added in the same manner, placing them between the tulle strips. The tulle ends may be knotted, trimmed diagonally, or trimmed to points.

MAKING THE BASIC POM-POM

To make the basic tulle pom-pom, you'll need a 12" length of 1/8"w ribbon for the tie, 6" lengths of 6" wide tulle (see individual projects for colors and amounts), ruler, and scissors (photo 6).

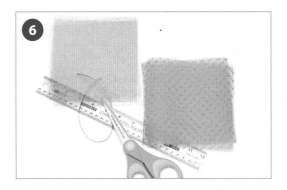

Stack the tulle squares and accordion pleat the tulle pieces. Securely tie the center with the ribbon (photo 7).

Being careful to not cut the ribbon ties, trim the pom-pom to the desired size (photo 8).

MAKING THE BASIC TOP

To make the basic top, you'll need a 22" square bandanna or a 24" fabric square, ⁷⁄₈" wide ribbon for the neck and back ties (see individual projects for color and amount), ⁷⁄₈" wide paper-backed fusible web tape, scissors, and an iron (photo 9).

If you are using a fabric square, follow the fusible web tape manufacturer's instructions to hem the fabric to approximately 22" square.

To make the neckline casing, lay the bandanna wrong side up on an ironing board and fuse web tape to the bandanna top point (photo 10). Fold the top point 8" to the wrong side and fuse (photo 11). Thread a 36" ribbon length through the neckline casing (photo 12).

For the back closure, fuse the web tape to the bandanna side points (photo 13). Fold the side points 3¹⁄₄" to the wrong side and fuse. Thread a 36" ribbon length through the casing on one side (photo 14). To wear the top, tie the neckline ribbon around the child's neck and thread the back closure ribbon through the opposite casing and tie the sides together.

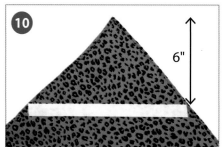
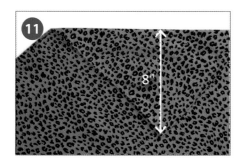
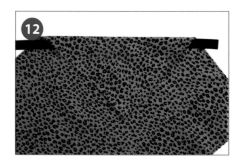
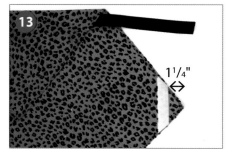
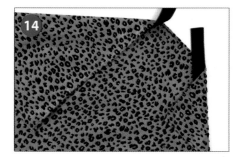

Production Team: Designer – Patti Wallenfang; Design Assistant – Kelly Reider; Technical Writer – Mary Sullivan Hutcheson; Technical Associates – Frances Huddleston, Lisa Lancaster, and Jean Lewis; Editorial Writer – Susan Frantz Wiles; Senior Graphic Artist – Lora Puls; Graphic Artist – Stacy Owens; Photostylist – Lori Wenger; Photographers – Jason Masters and Ken West.